I0471054

FIRE FREE WORK DAY

To Inspire You To 'Take Action'

RICHARD ABRAHAMS

A Special Thank You

This book would not have been possible without the support of a number of special people.

Firstly, I want to thank my beautiful fiancée Gillian, who has supported me and my family through this rollercoaster ride as I launch my new business. I love you more than could be expressed in this book, and thank you from the bottom of my heart for believing in my dream of delivering a 'Paradigm Shift in People and Business Development'.

Secondly, I want to thank Dean Jackson of 'I Love Marketing' (www.ILoveMarketing.Com). Dean is an amazing Marketing Genius. Dean has given me two amazing opportunities to learn with him and I dedicate this book to him for inspiring me and showing me how simple, yet powerful, writing a book could be. More specifically, how I can narrow my target market to such an extent that I could write a book specifically for them.

And finally three fantastic friends; Rob Lancaster, JJ Lynch and Andy Parton. You guys rock! Thank you for always being at the end of a phone or meeting up for a drink and a strategy chat. You always tell it to me straight and are all strong advocates for the success of my new business. Thank you for all your proof reading and adding some of your own personal insights into this book.

And there is always room for one more special thank you and that is to my children Charlotte, Daniel, Gabrielle and Benjamin and my extended family Jamie & Bradley. You make life so interesting and challenging. Balancing work life & family life is never easy, but thank you for supporting me in ways you may never realise... I hope I inspire you to succeed in life.

You are all absolutely special to me in supporting me in striving to take this new business to unrivalled new heights. Without all of your continuous support this would not have been possible, especially in this challenging time frame I set myself. I look forward to sharing my success with the people that mean the most to me. Thank you for being in my life!

THE FIRE FREE WORK DAY

Introduction

1 Day = 24 hours or 1440 minutes or 86,400 seconds. Nothing is going to change that. What you do with those hours, minutes and seconds, well that is a different story.

In this short read and MASSIVE 'TAKE ACTION' book, we are going to go deep into the causes of 'Fire Fighting', identify the facts and look at strategies to make changes and ultimately get you to 'TAKE ACTION' and get RESULTS. If you're up for that, keep reading!

How would you define 'Fire Fighting'?

Maybe simply, 'Spending More Time Reactively, Than Proactively'.

More often than not you find yourself indulged on the reactive rather than the proactive. When a number of things come together it's like a 'superstorm', any one on its own is enough to cause 'Fire Fighting', but all too often you get caught in the 'superstorms' of business life and it just spirals out of control. What you need to do is flip those reactive times into proactive times.

If your story begins with complete overwhelm, you feel like you are sinking, every now and again coming up for air, or you are just treading water going nowhere, well strap yourself in, buckle up, things are going to change for you... that is if, you are ready for change!

Is reading this book all it will take to put out the fires? No!

But you will have the foundations to build from and strategies to help you to extinguish the fires as and when they appear and then how to keep them away. How long it takes to extinguish your 'Fire Fighting', well that is down to how quickly you want change.

For some, you will be able to make changes instantly as you read the strategies in this book, others may take time to ponder on the strategies, digest them, contemplate whether they will work for you and then eventually 'Take Action'. And unfortunately for some of you, nothing is going to change because you haven't yet embraced the 'Five Keys To Success' (more about this later).

This book is designed to help you discover ways to ensure you extinguish your 'Fire Fighting' days, end the nonstop interruptions and stress of not being in control of your own day and become more proactive with your time. This book will guide you step by step through various strategies all designed to assist you in dealing with the many distractions we all get in our daily work lives.

As you start to read this book, the most important thing you will discover is 'Taking Action' and you have already started that process by reading this far.

We will cover lots of ways that you can improve your day, but all of them will require you to 'Take Action'. Don't think just reading the book will solve your 'Fire Fighting' issues. You need to be the one in the driving seat!

We all see the world differently, some will need to see quick wins, some will need a clear structure, some will need others to share the challenges with and some will need far more detail than we will cover in this short book. Whatever your style is, keep focused, keep motivated and keep reading and 'Taking Action'.

On that note let me just state, the book is designed to be a short read to ensure you can implement the strategies immediately. However, later in the book we will discuss how we should all seek continuous learning to ensure we improve our skills. Only when we accept that in order to grow we need to constantly keep learning will we be truly successful.

After each section there is a 'Take Action' box. Complete these 'Take Actions' by downloading the workbook at www.FireFreeWorkDay.Com/BookWorkbookDownload. This workbook will ensure you 'Take Action' and evidence results. You don't have to download the workbook to write up your 'Take Action' points, some of you might like to write your 'Take Action' points in the book, I won't be offended, in fact it is what I do when reading good books.

So if you are ready for change... It's time to don your fire jacket, go extinguish some fires and get down to action. By the end of the book you will be an effective 'Fire Fighter' and be sharing your success with others, helping them achieve what you have achieved, but remember YOU need to 'Take Action' at every step of this book. I think you are getting my key message... If not, here it is again: 'TAKE ACTION'.

Enjoy Reading, but more importantly enjoy 'Taking Action' and enjoy seeing RESULTS! (You must have got it by now...)

Richard Abrahams | CEO & Founder of TLC International Development

Author | Fire Free Work Day & Associated Product Suite

Having read many management training books and articles and watched and listened to hundreds of hours of personal development videos and audios over the past 30 years, some of the concepts and ideas from this book may relate back to great leaders and authors who have helped to develop my skills by understanding their philosophies of these topics.

Where possible I have tried to acknowledge these people in the book. All the content in this book has been written in my own words and my own understanding of these concepts and how they relate to 'Fire Fighting'. If I have inadvertently copied someone else's work, I apologise and would like to be informed so I can make amends.

Quick Guide To Getting Going

For some of you, the need to get results will be too great to read through this whole book right away before starting on some improvements.

You really do need to read the whole book to decide what will work best for you but if you just want a hint of what's in store, here is a summary of three quick tips to get you going.

Add Learning To Your Daily Routine

Just spending 12 minutes per day totally focused... that means no distractions whatsoever, turn off phones, put up a 'Busy' sign on the door, for just 12 minutes per day, that's it, learn one new topic or read one section of this book per day including 'Taking Action'.

12 minutes per day = 1 hour per week = 48 hours per year = 6 days of untapped learning and development every year. What would that do to help you learn how to put out your fires?

Time Blocking

You 'Block Time' in your diary for meetings and appointments, but you don't generally 'Block Time' for every task / project you plan to work on that week so you have little focus and no sense of urgency.

Plan your week in advance and 'Block Time' in your diary to complete your projects and tasks. Fill your diary up with 'Blocked Time' to do the most important task first and stick to the diary / plan.

One Page Plan

Create a daily 'One Page Plan' to ensure you focus completely on the top three tasks for that day. Ideally you should create your 'One Page Plan' as the last task of the day, that way when you go into work the next day, you know exactly what you need to do, before any distractions and before you open up your emails and get side tracked.

Five Keys To Success

Let's look at this 5* model you will need to embrace in order to get results... we call it The **'Five Keys To Success'**, you could also call it **'Life's Golden Nuggets'**. But let's do this slightly differently, let's talk about this in reverse, let's begin with the end in mind.

5. Results

Ultimately the end goal you will be looking for is that you get the results you desire back at work, you improve your strategies and you deal effectively with interruptions and distractions to ensure you remain focused on the key things that matter. You turn reactive activities into proactive activities and you see light at the end of the tunnel. So this is where we will start...and this becomes your end focus.

4. Action

In order to get the results you require you will need to 'Take Action'. Without 'Taking Action' it might sound obvious, but you won't get the results, so what stops you 'Taking Action'? YOU!!! Make sure you identify with this and embrace 'Taking Action'.

3. Potential

It's at this stage that the knowledge is injected, or the talent unleashed, this is where the learning takes place. If you don't feel you have the potential to succeed then you need to learn new skills, if you have the potential to succeed, then it just needs unleashing. The aim of this book is to deliver on both of these scenarios.

2. Attitude

Whether you need to learn a new skill or unleash your hidden talents, you need to have the right attitude to succeed. Attitude starts with the inner you, and your attitude to success is totally controlled by you. If you can't control your attitude, you can't succeed.

1. Belief

In order to have the right attitude, you need the belief that things will be better. So this is where 'YOU HAVE TO START' if you are going to ensure you get the results you require. You need to visualise success and believe that things will change. Start believing now!

A simple exercise to see 'Belief' in action is this… Stand up in the middle of a room facing a wall. Put one arm out (your writing arm) and point your finger at the wall in front of you. Without moving your feet, twist round as far as you can and notice where your finger is now pointing.

Don't read on any further than this if you have not done this yet, otherwise it will not work for you. You have to try this. Get up on your feet right now!

Now you are going to have to read these next few paragraphs, then try this next section… or get someone to read it out to you, as I am going to need you to close your eyes for this next bit…

Standing as you were before, arm raised, finger pointing, but with your eyes closed… **Visualise** your arm and body twisting round all the way to where you pointed to before, and then visualise it going a little bit further… Slowly visualise bringing your arm back to the beginning (N.B. Do not actually do it, just visualise it).

Then still with your eyes closed, again visualise your arm and body twisting round all the way to where you pointed before, and then where you went a little bit further and then visualise going a little further still... Slowly visualise bringing your arm back to the beginning.

Do this for one final time, visualise your arm and body twisting round all the way to where you pointed before, and then a little bit further and a little further still and then go a final little bit further still... Slowly visualise bringing your arm back to the beginning.

Now with your eyes open see how far round your arm goes this time...

I'm guessing it went a lot further than your original point of reference... Why?... Did I force it round... No! Did I stop you from going that far in the first place... No! What stopped you in the first stage was your belief.

You only visualised what going further would look like and created a sense of belief that you could do it.

Your **belief** gave you the right **attitude** to attempt to go further... that unleashed your **potential...** you took **action** and got **RESULTS**.

That is what is going to need to happen in this book if you want to get results, you have to start believing that things will change and start to 'Take Action'.

So to recap on these 'Five Keys To Success'...

If any of these stages are missing you will not get the desired response you require, so ask yourself, do you **believe** that you have the right **attitude** and **potential** to learn from this book and will take immediate **action**?

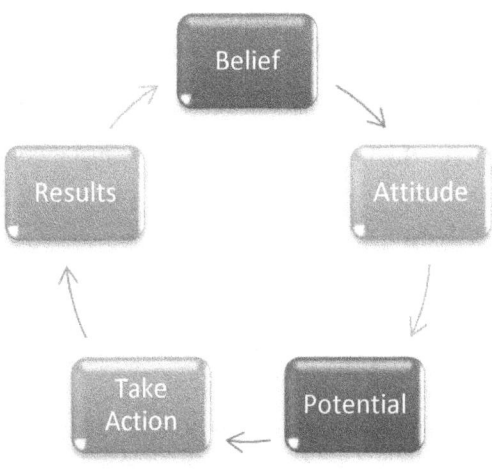

If you answered yes to those four stages, then I can assure you that you will get the fifth stage... **results**. If you answered no to any of the first four, then that is what you will need to address before you read any further.

Once you start seeing **results**, this will fuel your desire to **believe** more in your **potential**, and that will change your **attitude** for success, which in turn will open up your **potential** further and get you to take more **Action** and that will get you even more **results**. So hopefully you can see 'WHY' these 'Five Keys to Success' are so vital in you moving forward.

For your own sake do not read any further if you have not bought into the 'Five Keys To Success'. If you do **believe** you have the right **attitude** and **potential** to learn from this book, then **'Take Action'** by turning over this page and watch the **results** flood in.

The Early Signs

What Causes 'Fire Fighting'?

All too often you can find yourself 'reacting' to situations you are faced with. There can be many reasons that you find yourself 'Fire Fighting', some of the most widely talked about are (The Big Six);

1. Email

    -   Too many emails each day, emails with no impact on your end results, people expecting an instant response to their email.

2. Telephone

    -   The phone keeps ringing, people keep calling with trivial things they could be dealing with themselves, customers querying their orders.

3. People

    -   People keep interrupting, they want to know how to do this, how to do that, they keep changing their minds.

4. Yourself

    -   Your own thoughts, your mind wanders thinking of all the good things that need doing and all the not so good things that need doing, it never rests.

5. Projects

- Too many projects to deal with, you seem to have five times as many projects as you did last year, your projects go on and on, with no end in sight.

6. Time

- Not enough hours in the day, you get up early, leave late, and you still do not get everything done because of all of the above issues.

Understanding what is causing your 'Fire Fighting' issues is a great place to start. You can so easily get caught in the 'OCD Loop' (Obsessive Compulsive Disorder), where you find yourself checking emails as they come in, looking for that next lead or sale.

Answering the phone just in case you miss an important call, only to find out someone wants to sell you something you don't need. People popping by your desk for no specific reason, just to have a chat.

You find yourself thinking about lots of projects; new and old, and then all of a sudden the email notification box comes up and you go to check that urgent (or not) email and the 'OCD Loop' starts all over again.

Eliminating the issues of the 'BIG SIX' causes; well that's what you will aim to do by the end of this book.

Take Action: *List every other reason that causes you to 'Fire Fight' as this will make it easier to decide how to prevent going backwards from now on.*

What It Does To You?

There are many ways 'Fire Fighting' affects you, here's just a few;

1. Feeling stressed at work or at home;
2. Non productive days;
3. Targets not being reached;
4. Projects not completed on time;
5. Health, sickness or tiredness;
6. Arguments with colleagues;
7. No promotion or career development.

All of these, and many other side effects, will cause you to feel pressured and will most probably result in you underperforming which will create even more pressure and more under performance.

'Fire Fighting' should come with the same government health warning that you get on cigarettes...

- WARNING! 'FIRE FIGHTING' WILL SERIOUSLY DAMAGE YOUR HEALTH...
- QUITTING 'FIRE FIGHTING' NOW GREATLY REDUCES SERIOUS RISKS TO YOUR HEALTH...

Take Action: Identify what 'Fire Fighting' is really doing to you. Be honest with yourself, even if you don't want to write it down. Identifying what it is doing to you and really acknowledging this will give you the right 'Attitude' to make a difference. Say to yourself 'This has to stop right now'!

How Do You Know?

The Tell Tale Signs That You Are Fighting Fires

Some signs are visible, but many signs are also invisible, these can include;

1. A piling system on your desk - Visible

2. Lots of unfinished projects on the go – Visible / Invisible

3. Going from one meeting to another - Visible

4. Constant switching from one task to another – Visible / Invisible

5. Unbalanced day - Invisible

Take Action: *List all your 'Fire Fighting' issues. Make it a no holds barred contest, ask your colleagues what they see, write down absolutely everything that is causing you to not be in control. Track how long you spend online each day, by online I mean email, internet etc. When you track your online usage you can then quickly see how much time is spent 'online' vs. 'working on projects'.*

Where To Start Your Journey

Visualise What A Magic Wand Can Do For You

If you could raise a magic wand and say goodbye to all your 'Fire Fighting' issues what would it look like? An interesting question... but actually a really important question to ask yourself. If you can't visualise what it will look like when you can overcome your 'Fire Fighting' issues, how will you ever know when you are there.

Take Action: Take two minutes and find a place of peace and quiet. Sit in a comfy chair, close your eyes, take a few deep breaths in and out and take yourself on a journey of self awareness. Create a picture of perfection, list what you would see, feel, hear if things were running like clockwork. Trust me, this is a must if you really want to get rid of your 'Fire Fighting' issues. Write a one page document outlining your visualisation.

Acknowledge That Things Need To Change

You've just created a vision of perfection, so you know what it will look like when you succeed. The next step you need to deal with is acknowledging that you want things to change. It can't just be 'I would like to'..., it needs to be 'I WILL DO WHATEVER IT TAKES TO GET RESULTS'.

It really isn't worth your time continuing to read this book if you are not fully committed to change. I know that sounds harsh, but I want you to succeed.   In order to succeed you have to have the right attitude, the right frame of mind and the total commitment for success.

If now is not the right time for you, that's ok, you can always come back to this when you are fully committed. If you have the right attitude, let's move on.

Take Action: Write a clear statement of your intentions, why you are committed this time, what you will do to stay committed, what will happen when the world tries to put *obstacles in your way to stop you achieving your goals and how you will remain focused.*

Commit That You Will Change

If you know things need to change then you have to ask yourself, what will stop you from changing? This is where you go back to the 'Five Keys To Success' and stages 1 & 2 (Belief and Attitude). If these are not aligned, then you will struggle to ever take control of your 'Fire Fighting' issues.

Ask yourself what will stop you committing to getting rid of your 'Fire Fighting'? What are your fears and frustrations? Tackle these head on, because if you want results you will have to accept change and commit to change.

Don't do yourself an injustice, spend as much time as needed to go back over these first few paragraphs to ensure your 'Belief and Attitude' are aligned. If they are not aligned, do yourself a favour and drop us an email at info@tlcinternationaldevelopment.com or schedule a call using our 'Schedule a Consultation' system on our website www.tlcinternationaldevelopment.com and we'll see if we can help you so you can fully benefit from this book.

Take Action: This is a big step, make sure you accept that change is needed and you are committed to change, otherwise you won't get the results you require. Clearly outline why this time is different, how committed are you to really tackle your 'Fire Fighting' issues, if you were to score this out of 100, what is your commitment level? I am guessing you are somewhere in the 60 – 80%, what can you do, what do you need to do to get into the 90% - 100% level? Clearly outline your commitment to change.

Set Your Standards – Score Your Standards

Knowing who you are and what you stand for is paramount in setting your standards high. If you want to rid yourself of your 'Fire Fighting' issues then you need to set yourself standards that you live by and you won't deviate from. If you were to set three standards that you live by as a person and three standards you live by when connecting with people, what would they be and why?

The three standards that I live by as a person are;

1. Enthusiasm

    a. I want to always be enthusiastic in every aspect of my life. I know enthusiasm is infectious and when I am totally enthusiastic I enthuse those around me, this in turn makes me feel great about myself and that in turn creates even more enthusiasm.

    b. People generally might put out 50% of the enthusiasm that you put out. If you want them to increase their enthusiasm, then you will need to increase your enthusiasm.

2. Presence

    a. My thinking style is naturally very creative and as such this makes me easily distracted, which in turn means I am not always focused on the task to hand. To fully engage in the projects, tasks, and connections with people, I need to be totally focused. I do this by ensuring I am totally present when working on projects / tasks and when connecting with people.

b. When I am fully present, I feel vibrant, I feel alive and ready to contribute, so I am always checking in with myself and asking what level of presence am I right now?

3. Boldness

a. Bold comes in two forms, one is how I appear and the other is how I behave. Firstly appearance... I like to make a great first impression, this takes form in how I dress, how I look and how I feel. To be bold in all of these areas I need to be happy with who I am. When I look good I will feel good.

b. Secondly, is how I behave... Those that know me personally know I do not swear, I take people for who they are and I am not afraid to speak out (in a polite way of course). In accepting everyone for who they are (let's face it we all breathe the same air and flush out the same waste), it ensures I stand out as a respected leader.

The three standards that I live by when connecting with others are;

1. Caring

    a. Everyone has a story, and everyone's lives are different, in accepting people for who they are, where they came from and what they stand for they all have different agendas to mine. That doesn't mean my agenda is right... just different, when I care for other peoples agendas as well as my own, it makes me a more engaging and caring person.

    b. Caring for other people is top of my agenda as I get great pleasure from unleashing talents in people, teaching them new skills, coaching them and watching them grow. This in turn fuels my passion for growth, it's a win win for me.

2. Engaging

    a. When people feel a sense of engagement with you, they are more likely to open up and support what you stand for. If you just come across as me, me, me without giving anything back, people are unlikely to engage with you.

b.   I always look at giving people three times the value back that they give to me, I don't always reach that goal, but I strive for it, and it shows that person that I am totally committed to them.

3.   Inspiring

a.   There are many people that inspire me and fuel my passion for success and in return I look for people that I can inspire, to help and support their success. I don't think of myself as the cleverest person in the room, but I do like being in a room of clever people and inspiring them to greatness.

b.   When I inspire people, I get a great amount of pride in what I do. It allows me to connect at a deeper level and it allows for my growth as well as others. When you see that light bulb moment in someone else's eyes, it's like a new born baby being brought into the world. I live to inspire!

So I have 6 standards that I live by and in each and every one of these, I am constantly scoring myself on a scale of 1 – 10. When I feel myself dropping below a 10, I tell myself, *'these are my standards, I own them and it is my responsibility to ensure I am performing at a 10,* now what do I need to do to raise my game today?'

Take Action: What are your three standards as a person? What is your current score in each of these? What are your three standards when connecting with people? What is your current score in each of these? Decide how you will reinforce these standards on a daily / hourly basis to ensure you are performing as close to a 10 as possible.

Start Day

Knowing when to start can be a tough decision. You are either going to be one of those people who have already started, or you are going to need time to get going. If you are the latter, set a day, say a week or two weeks from today to put aside as a 'Planning Day'.

Only start when you are fully committed to change, not just when you would like to start. You have to be 100% ready... It's like an aeroplane waiting to take off. There's no point taxiing down the runway and expecting to be up in the air, it will only end in misery... You need full throttle in order to take off.

If you are not yet at full throttle keep reading through the book, but be ready to launch into action on your set 'Start Day' as soon as you feel ready to take off.

Take Action: Choose a start date. Tell everyone this is your start date. Look forward to your start date and start on your start date 100% committed to success!

Make Time In Your Day To Plan

You already know that time is very precious and you can't turn back time, so you have to make time in your day to plan to start, plan to plan and plan to deliver. At first this will be tough and you will struggle to keep it up. The key is consistency. In time you will reflect back and feel very proud of what you have achieved.

Depending at what level you take this initially, you will need to dedicate regular time to plan. It may be 10 minutes or 30 minutes or more each day, the amount is irrelevant, the consistency is what counts. As you dedicate consistent time to this, you will see results... Results will encourage you to take more action, reach more potential, fuel your attitude and strengthen your belief, which will result in a loop back to the beginning again.

Take Action: Decide how long you will spend planning each day, commit to an amount of time that you can feasibly achieve and do it consistently.

Fire Free Time System

Look to balance your days and weeks, consisting of a mixture of **Action Days**, **Preparation Days**, **Buffer Days** and **Free Days**. Getting a structure to your days and weeks will help you to plan more effectively whilst also ensuring you remain in control. It is very easy to get distracted by your surroundings, but when you know your optimal performance strategies for each of these days, you can ensure your environment is optimal for that day to get improved results.

Having structured days will ensure you get a balance to your days. It will allow you to get in the right frame of mind for each of the types of days to ensure you remain focused at the optimal performance level.

If you don't have these planned days in your diary, what often happens is you find yourself flicking from one type of day to another and not working at your optimum performance level.

The Fire Free Time System consists of;

- **Action Days** – An Action Day is being 100% present, where you clearly know the tasks and projects that need working on. An Action Day is a money making day or dealing with those activities that generate results.

- **Preparation Days** – A Preparation Day is exactly what it states. A Preparation Day comes before an Action Day and is for all the preparation work needed to ensure you can have an Action Day with no distraction.

- **Back Up Days** – A Back Up Day should be scheduled weekly and used to work on strategic direction, delegation and dealing with those little things that always need doing, the sort of things that stop you doing the other three days.

- **Free Days** – You don't usually block in Free Days, you just look forward to the weekends that you get off... If and when you get them! Free Days are a must for rejuvenating yourself. When you block in Free Days and ensure you take them, you will benefit in the long run.

It will be too easy to block in a Free Day, then at the first opportunity give it up because you have too much work on. But like all these other concepts, when you truly dedicate yourself to them, you will get amazing benefits from it, but you will only find that out when you try it.

In time you will aim to get more balance, creating more focus and free days in your routine.

Take Action: Decide in your own mind what your Action Day, Preparation Day, Back Up Day and Free Day will look like. In order to perform at your optimum performance level, decide what Action Days, Preparation Days, Back Up Days or Free Days you need to schedule for your current projects and tasks. Block these in your diary and stick to the plan. i.e. Today is my 'X' day and I will only focus on my 'X' day. You can break these days down into half days or quarter days, the key is the structure of the day.

Share Your Journey – Get Support From Your Team

What you're about to embark on, let's face it is a MASSIVE CHALLENGE for you. If it wasn't a massive challenge you would be dealing with this effectively already. For this to really work for you the strategies in this book have to become habitual.

Habits don't happen over night or at the flick of a switch. For something to become a habit you need to consistently practise these strategies over at least 30 days. If you don't commit 100% you will not get back 100%. What you commit % wise is what you will get back.

These strategies are most probably going to stretch you outside your comfort zone. What does that feel like?... Try switching your watch from whatever wrist it is on to the other wrist... I'm guessing that already feels uncomfortable. But keep it there... And every day from now on put it on the new wrist. It is going to take a long time before this becomes a habit or feels comfortable but you need to consistently remind yourself why you are doing this. It will be the same for these strategies, don't expect them to work after one or two attempts, you have to consistently apply them.

A really beneficial way for you to succeed at 'Fire Fighting' is to get the support of your team, colleagues, friends and family. They are pivotal to your success. If they know what you are doing and how you are focusing on specific strategies, they are more likely to bother you less at times they know you are focused.

The other reason why it is good to have them support you is for accountability. When you are left to your own devices, it is so easy to fall back into old habits, but when someone holds you accountable and challenges and motivates you, that will drive you to success.

Take Action: Having your team on board to your strategies is critical to your success. Communicate in an effective way to your team, outlining not just the 'What & How' of what you are doing, but more importantly the 'Why'. Explain how critical to your success they are.

One Step At A Time

As with making a consistent time in your day, achieving one step at a time will demonstrate results to you, which will also fuel the loop back to the 'Five Keys To Success'.

It is far better to achieve one thing, than fail at lots of things. Choose your most important task and complete that before you complete any other task. It sounds simple, but most people get distracted and end up working on lots of things at the same time.

Ask yourself... 'What MUST I COMPLETE TODAY'? Make that your mission for the day?

Take Action: Ask yourself 'What must I complete today...?' At the beginning of everyday day ask yourself the same question.

Be 10% Better Than Your Average Colleagues

At the beginning of the book we talked about the parts **'Belief'** and **'Attitude'** play in moving you forward. Another great strategy is looking at your colleagues and setting yourself the goal to be 10% better than the average person you work with.

Take a look at what these people are good at, how they perform, how they are perceived and the results they get, then imagine what being 10% better would look like.

Use this drive to propel yourself as the leading edge in leadership. Teach other people your newly learnt skills and share success with colleagues and friends, this in turn will propel you forward as the 'go to' person for dealing with 'Fire Fighting' issues and you will become 10% better than your colleagues.

Take Action: Take a look at the people who surround you... Look at their skills and decide what being 10% better would look like. Then go for it!

M.O.T.

An M.O.T. test is all about an annual full health check for your vehicle. It's a time when every component of the car is put under scrutiny and there are strict guidelines that have to be met if your car is to pass.

Creating your own M.O.T. for your business will ensure you regularly check every aspect of your business, looking at whether that specific aspect meets or exceeds expectations and what areas are faulty and need replacing.

Breaking every part of your business into mini processes will help you to fine tune your business and also identify where parts are not working properly, for example answering the phone, how many rings (as a standard) before anyone answers it? What is the greeting message? Your invoicing process, when are they sent? How are they followed up? How do you thank customers for payment? How do you acknowledge receipt of payment?

The key is to identify what is running at a 5* level and what is running below a 5* level. What is running smoothly, what is causing you to 'Fire Fight' and where can you improve the performance to free up more time for other stuff.

Dash Board

If you consider a car dashboard, you have certain key features that help propel the car forward or stop it from accidents. You can use this concept to create a dashboard for your own business.

Having a dashboard can help you understand the direction you are going, keep you focused on the vision ahead, whilst putting every aspect into perspective. With a clear focus that will ultimately result in less 'Fire Fighting'.

Once you have gone through this exercise you might never look at the dashboard of your car in the same light, I know every time I get in the car, it instantly reminds me of all of these aspects and keeps me focused on the goals ahead.

These are some areas of the dashboard to relate your business to;

- **Windscreen** – How clear is your vision?
- **GPS** – Where are you going?
- **Steering Wheel** – Which direction do you need to turn now?

- **Rear View Mirror** – Looking back where have you come from?
- **Speedometer** – How fast are you currently moving?
- **RPM** – How smoothly is the business running?
- **Accelerator Pedal** – How fast do you want to inject pace into the business?
- **Brake Pedal** – What are the areas that you need to stop and rethink?
- **Clutch Pedal** – What do you need to do to engage a change of direction?
- **Indicators** – Who do you need to tell your direction too?
- **Airbags** – What is your strategy for emergencies?
- **Air Vents** – How do you keep all staff motivated and engaged?
- **Stereo** – What advertising do you need?

Take Action: *Create your own business dashboard, what does it tell you? What areas are you currently 'Fire Fighting'? If you were to score each area 1 – 10, what would be your average score? What areas are scoring below a 7 and what can you do to correct this?*

Wheel Of Life

Life is not just about business and in order to balance out your work life with your personal life, you need to look at the bigger picture and how all these different factors affect your performance. Creating a 'Wheel Of Life' is a really powerful exercise and one I truly recommend, because as you go through this exercise you will quickly see how balanced or unbalanced your life really is, and where you can focus on improvements.

The wheel of life can be as simple or as complex as you choose. You start with categories of your life, e.g. Work, Family, Health, Finance, and then you add in other areas as you see fit, e.g. Vision, Community, Social Life and Education. An example of one is below.

Once you have decided on all the categories that fill up your 'Wheel Of Life', you should then score where you think you are in each of these areas. For example I have scored a 3 in 'Health' as I know that is a current focus of mine.

Once you have scored yourself in each of the categories, plot them on your own graph by drawing a dot on the graph with 10 being on the outer edge and 1 on the inner edge. Once all of these are plotted, then connect the dots...

In an ideal world a balanced approach would be great and would look like a smooth (ish) circle, but what you have most probably found is, if you were able to roll your 'Wheel Of Life' down a steep hill, it would clang and chunk its way down, in not a very smooth way.

Take Action: Decide on your categories (or use these), then plot where you are now. What do you need to do to smooth out your wheel? Be honest with yourself, just like I scored myself a 3 in health at the time of writing this book, you are more likely to take responsibility for what needs doing in your life if you are totally honest with yourself about where you currently are now. Now decide what you need to do to move your score up by just one point in each category. Visualise what a 10 would be like, but today aim to be one point better than you were yesterday. When you master that point, move up another point, but just focus on one point at a time.

Let's take this concept one stage further and create a 'Business Only' 'Wheel of Life'. It may look something like this;

<figure>*Take Action: Once again decide on the categories that suit you or feel free to choose these and put a score of 1 – 10 in each of these categories. Be honest, it is the only way to grow.*</figure>

Know Your Facts First

As you are still reading this... there is still hope for you. We're nearly at the start of the '30 Tips'. This next section really builds the foundations to solve your 'Fire Fighting' issues.

Knowing your facts will help you to decide how drastically you need to 'Take Action' consistently, which areas you can get a few quick wins in, and how you can develop a long term strategy to move forward.

Where Do You Spend Your Time?

There are only 168 hours per week for you to deal with ABSOLUTELY everything in your life and that includes sleeping, eating, etc. You most probably don't have a real sense of where this time goes, it just seems like Groundhog Day every day... you get up, get dressed, eat, go to work, spend time with your family, go to bed and so starts the next day.

Having a really clear understanding of where you are spending all of your time NOW, and where you really want to spend your time IN FUTURE, I'm guessing will be two different answers.

So let's get a real understanding on where your 168 hours per week are being used currently and where you would like them to be used in the future. You can use this simple chart to guide you or create your own, you will also need to add in your own categories, but here are a few as an example.

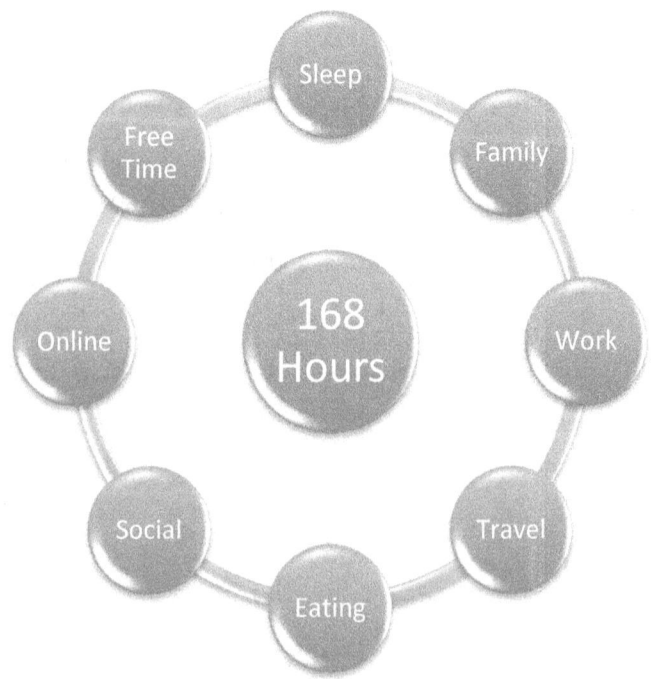

First, calculate how much time you currently spend in each of these areas, or on your own categories that you have decided on. N.B. You might only be able to do this as a rough guide, but try to average it out to what a standard / normal week looks like for you.

Write that number down above each category, it should add up to 168 hours. Now calculate how much time you want to be spending on each of these categories in twelve months time and write that number down below each category, it should also add up to 168 hours.

If you don't get to 168 hours in either charts, go back and see what category is missing until you get to 168 hours.

Take Action: Calculate where you spend your time? What surprises did you get from this exercise? Where are the big differences? What are you willing to do about these? What needs to happen now to get you your 'In Future' figures?

What Are Your Time Robbers?

You have things that rob your time, from distractions like email, phones, people and your own mind wandering. But what about if you got right down to the minute detail, what would you uncover?

You might see things like, losing interest in a task, over thinking, things on your desk, distractions from people around you, lack of priority, surfing on the internet or attention span.

Understanding what is robbing you of your time is key to deciding how to deal with it. It is only when you fully accept what is robbing your time that you can then decide on a course of action to stop these 'Time Robbers' from affecting you in the future.

For example if email notifications cause you to stop what you are doing to see what just came into your inbox when you are in 'Focus Time', then just turning off your notification box or closing your email down during these 'Focus Times' will benefit you greatly.

Likewise if flittering from one project on your desk to another when you get bored with the one you are working on robs your time, just clearing your desk of all projects apart from the one you are working on will help you to remain focused.

Take Action: Be honest with yourself... Get a sheet of paper and draw a line down the middle. On the left side write out all of your 'Time Robbers', numbering them 1 – whatever number you get to (try to get to at least 10+), go into as much detail as possible. Now on the right hand side next to each 'Time Robber', write out what action you need to take to rid yourself of that 'Time Robber'. Then create a plan to ensure you stop these 'Time Robbers'.

Track Your Day

It's time to see what actually happens during your working week. What you need to do is track your day in 15 minute sections (Time Logging). In the workbook you will find a daily and weekly 'Time Logging' page, but you can easily create your own if you choose.

The key is to 'CONSISTENTLY' record everything you do on a normal day to day routine. Recording these activities in 15 minute intervals would be beneficial, if you don't want this much detail (I strongly suggest you do) you can record them in 30 minute intervals. You need to do this consistently for a week (minimum) or two weeks (preferred) to fully understand the picture and to benefit in the long run. Set a timer that goes off every 15 minutes to remind you to log what you have just done. The more accurate the log, the more you will benefit in understanding the areas you need to improve.

I appreciate it is going to seem laborious in the beginning, but the rewards you will reap in the long term will far outweigh the initial inconvenience. This information will help you to align your systems and improve your performance.

Take Action: Log all your tasks daily in 15 minute intervals for the next two weeks.

Join The Dots

Now you have logged everything you have done over the past two weeks (and if you haven't done that yet, please do it now), if you were holding each 15 minute task like they were a deck of cards, do you have a hand of similar tasks logged together?

Are all of your phone calls batched together? All of your project preparation times together? All of your action times together? You are really looking at this with a fine tooth comb. It's all about making the best use of your time. So take your time to see where this all fits together.

If all of your 'Preparation Work' times were batched together, all of your 'Action Time' batched together etc, you would be running nearly as effectively as a Formula 1 car. When you look at F1, (and I am an avid follower), their attention to detail on the small things and their focus on the large things are what makes them so effective. When everything is running at maximum performance then you too will be running on all cylinders.

If you find yourselves flicking from one task to another when you could have joined the dots and batched the work together, that's when you'll find yourself performing at a far reduced pace. That is what will ultimately eat up your time and cause you to 'Fire Fight' more often than not.

By batching tasks together at specific times for specific jobs (Time Batching) you will soon see an increase in your performance and a decrease in your time wastage. Imagine it is like a production line for efficiency, what will joining the dots tell you about your production line?

Take Action: Go through your 'Time Log' looking for where you could 'Batch' similar tasks together. Redraw your Time Log with these 'Time Batched' tasks together and then trial this new approach.

Identify Leaks

It is easy to identify leaks in water pipes when they are visible, (there is normally water dripping or flooding out), but you also need to identify when there is a leak that is invisible. Like if your pipe is buried underground, you might only notice the leak by the cost of your water bill going up or the pressure going down. This is much harder to identify.

Instead of water flowing through your pipe, imagine that 'Time' is flowing through your pipes. It is the same with your business, you first need to identify where there might be leaks in your systems and processes that are visible as well as when they might be invisible, only then can you work out how to plug all those leaks.

A temporary fix is just that and eventually the leak will reappear and sometimes a whole new piece of piping will need to be installed. It is the same in business... it is better to identify and deal with the leak than to let it get worse and have to replace it.

Leaks

Take Action: Take time to really identify what is causing the leaks both visible and invisible and put a permanent solution in place. Stop fixing tasks with sticky plasters once and for all! Ask your colleagues where they see your leaks? Identifying now where potential future leaks might appear will also be very beneficial.

List All Of Your Projects

Well I'm guessing it might seem obvious, but you need to get a full list of every project or tasks in both your business life and personal life. Now one great way to do this can be found on page 42 **'Focus Time'**. Whether you choose to check that page out or just get a pen and paper and start writing, you need to get ABSOLUTELY everything written down.

Without a clear picture of what you have on your plate, you will not be in a position to move forward as without having everything listed as you work your way through your list the other things you did not list will keep coming back to haunt you. So be clear, 'Everything' is 'Everything' no matter how small or trivial it may seem at the moment.

Project 1	Project 2	Project 3
• Task 1	• Task 1	• Task 1
• Task 2	• Task 2	• Task 2
• Task 3	• Task 3	• Task 3
• Task 4	• Task 4	• Task 4
• Task 5	• Task 5	• Task 5
• Task 6	• Task 6	• Task 6

Take Action: *Write down every task both business and personal. Break the tasks down into bite size tasks. For all you list loving people this tip will be like candy in a sweet shop. If you're not the list loving person then let me just say the extra effort put in here will be so beneficial to you.*

Assign A £ Sign To What You Do

An easy way to understand the value of the projects / tasks you are working on is to assign a '£' value and an 'importance' value and then balance up the pro's and con's of prioritising them.

You see it could be a really important task but has a low financial reward for YOU, or a high financial reward for you but of low importance to the business, either way you need to weigh up the pros and cons, deciding where it fits in YOUR PERSONAL priority order or where it fits in YOUR BUSINESS priority order.

This will show you where you need to keep your focus, where you can delegate and where you MUST complete a task. It also shows you the reward you will get completing the task or project and the benefit to you and the business.

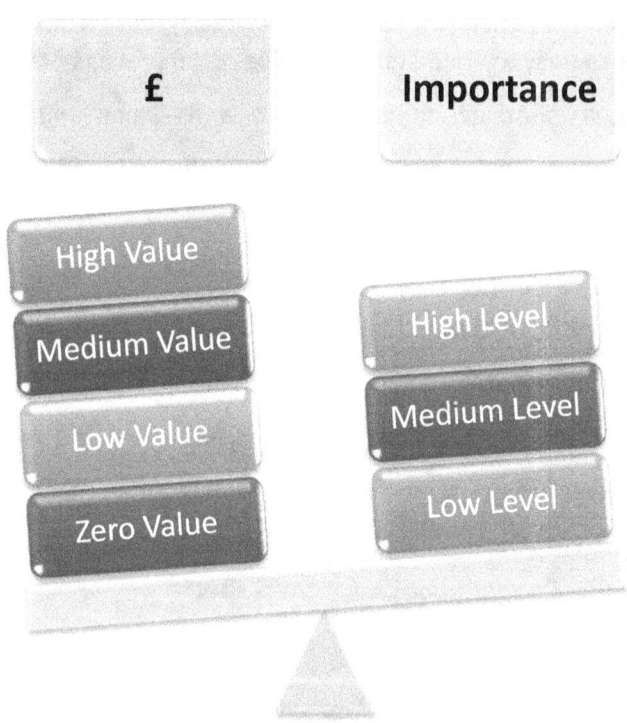

Take Action: List a '£' amount and 'Importance' amount to every project or task you have in your list or you add to your list, even the ones you don't end up doing.

Score Your Projects

Knowing where to start a long list of projects and tasks can seem daunting. Scoring your projects and tasks will help sort out the priority order and categorising them.

Starting with the full list of tasks and projects you identified in 'List All Of Your Projects', go through the list and start to categorise them, putting the following letters 'A', 'B', 'C', 'D' or 'E' next to every item;

A. Action Now - Urgent & Important

   i.   Needs to be done today

   ii.   Very important to your business

   iii.   Serious consequences if not completed

   iv.   Complete before any other task or project is started

B. Block Time - Important but Not Urgent

   i.   Does not need to be done today

   ii.   Needs to done by X

   iii.   Consequences if not completed

iv.   Block the correct amount of time in your diary to complete the task or project

v.   Might mean blocking time tomorrow, next week, next month... it is just important to block time

C. Choice – Rewarding but Not Important

i.   Rewarding to do if you have time

ii.   No real consequences if you do it or not

iii.   Block time into your day for the rewarding to do things. N.B. Only if 'A' tasks are completed and no 'B' task are due that day

iv.   It is always rewarding to do things you like doing, so try to treat yourself as often as possible

D. Delegate - Urgent but Not Important

i.   Not important to you but important to the business

ii.   Delegate to someone else

E. Eliminate - Not Urgent & Not Important

i.   No consequences to you or the business

ii. Completely remove from your list

Once you have all the 'A', 'B', 'C', 'D' or 'E's listed, you will then need to prioritise each of these categories prioritising them further listing them A1, A2, B1, B2 etc

'A' tasks can cause you to 'Fire Fight'... They are not planned like a 'B' task and as such have an impact on your planning and being in control of your time.

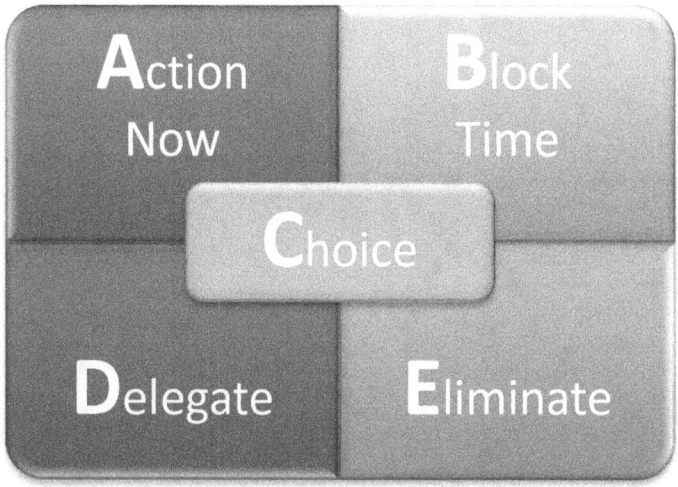

N.B. Never do a 'B' task when there is an 'A' task waiting!

Take Action: *Go through your entire list painstakingly putting an A, B, C, D or E on your list, then go through and add a priority order i.e. A1, A2, A3 etc. This may take you some time to do but again it is important to emphasise what is going on... what needs doing... and what needs working on NOW! By identifying your 'D' and 'E' tasks you can quickly remove them from your list in the correct manner... Delegating or Eliminating.*

30 Tips To Ensure You Get Results

The following 30 tips will help you improve and ultimately extinguish all your 'Fire Fighting' issues. Just one tip might make a significant impact to your day, and here you have 30 tips to work through. The tips are in no particular order, but there should be some tips here even for those professional 'Fire Fighters' who only get caught out every now and again.

Read through all the tips and decide which ones / combinations will work for you. You might trial some only to find out that it doesn't really suit your style, that's ok. You will find some tips or combinations of tips that will really get your mind going and will fit in with your style. You might adapt these strategies to suit your needs. Whatever you do, the key always goes back to WILL YOU 'TAKE ACTION'? You have to start somewhere so start with a commitment and a time frame to put this into action. You need to decide which ones you can work with and which ones you can't.

Tip 1 - Two Week Test

Commit yourself unreservedly to a two week test. The more committed to change, the more you will be willing to give time to these strategies. Decide at what level you want to start this 'change' process;

a. **Master** - Apply as many strategies as possible. Embed them until they become 'habit'. At this level you will look for every opportunity to embed these strategies.

b. **Advanced** - Apply five to ten strategies as soon as possible embedding them all day long until they become a 'habit'.

c. **Intermediate** - Apply one to five strategies and allow 4 hours per day to embed these strategies. For the rest of the day you continue as normal.

d. **Beginner** – Apply one strategy at a time and allow 2 hours per day to embed this strategy. For the rest of the day you continue as normal.

You might have noticed that these levels started with the highest level first. Why? If you really want to overcome these 'Fire Fighting' issues then you need to totally commit to the process, however choose the right level for you.

Take Action: Decide which level you want to start at. Start at a level that is suitable for you, you can always move up or down a level as required. Choose the level you believe will be the easiest to commit to and start there. However if you are the ambitious 'go getter' decide on the best option, then move up one level and start there instead. i.e. If you feel you could easily start at the 'Intermediate' level, then move up to the 'Advance' level.

Tip 2 - Email Filtering Rules

Let's look at an area that affects everyone, apart from those who don't 'Fire Fight'. If you can clear out your inbox from the many distractions it causes you, would that be a good place to start?

What you need is a simple way to keep your inbox under control and let's face it, some people get 200 – 600+ emails a day. If each email took just 10 seconds to read, act on (if needed) and filed, that is still around 33 – 100 minutes to clear your inbox and you know it takes longer than 10 seconds on average, but I think you get the point.

You can create email filtering rules to automatically file certain emails straight into folders without them hitting your inbox. You still would have access to them, you don't lose them and they can still be read in the 'Unread' folder. That would certainly improve your inbox and is simple to set up.

I go to this folder once a day and can easily scan through the many emails in there in a matter of seconds, moving any to the inbox if needed. Once you mark them all as read, they are already filed, so you only handled them once. Trust me, this is a game changer if you get a lot of emails.

Take Action: Check out your email system to learn how to create filter rules for your inbox. Every day you get emails that are not urgent or important, create a filter rule for them. Each day you will see your inbox get emptier and emptier, leaving only the important and urgent emails to deal with. You can always reverse any filters rules. GAME CHANGER!

Tip 3 - G.O.L.F

A great strategy to get you in the right frame of mind to complete your tasks without distraction is start to play G.O.L.F, by the way that's not on the fairway, but in the 'headway'. Dean Jackson (www.ILoveMarketing.Com) first explained this concept to me and this is how I could see that it could fit into your 'Fire Fighting' strategy.

- Goal

  o Start to play your G.O.L.F one goal at a time. When you play golf you start at hole 1 and work your way round to hole 18 and finally onto the 19th hole (drink house). It should be the same with your projects and tasks, working your way through them one goal (hole) at a time. This will ensure you remain structured, focused and get results, whilst still leaving time for your 19th hole.

- Optimal Environment

  o When I am writing books or designing training courses, I like my desk cleared of all distractions, no access to internet, with just my laptop, pen, paper and a timer. When I am strategising or brainstorming I like a large central desk, plain walls (for sticking things too), my flipchart, whiteboard and lots of open space to pace up and down. When I am studying / reading, I like nothing more than just my large sofa or my padded reclining office chair, with my feet up.

- Limited Distraction

  o For me to have limited distraction I need to be in a place with no other distractions, no internet, no people, no phones, no music. It may sound like hell, but actually it is the only way I don't get distracted. By distracted, I mean by other people, by incoming mail, by phone calls but more importantly by 'MWS' (mind wandering syndrome).

- Fixed Time Frame

  o When you play golf, cricket or go to the theatre or movies etc, you know for that fixed time you are not going to do anything else. It's the same with projects and tasks. When I know the time frame I am working to, I have an end in mind and a goal to aim for. If I set a target for that timeframe, it ensures I stay focused and don't sway off the path,

but still have an end in mind to look forward too.

Take Action: Decide on your G.O.L.F. strategy? Get your
G.O.L.F. strategy right and it will set you up for results.
*Decide to tackle each **G**oal 'one at a time'. Decide what is*
*your **O**ptimal environment for getting things done? Decide*
*how to **L**imit your distractions? Decide what is your optimal*
***F**ixed time frame before you get distracted?*

Tip 4 - Focus Time

Imagine you were going to play golf or going to the theatre.
In the 'During' time, you are unlikely to respond to emails,
answer a call or speak to other people, unless you want to
be rude! You need to apply the same 'Focus Time' to deal
with all your tasks. Later on we will be talking about the
50:10 rule, but for this exercise you need to find just 50
minutes of total focus time to complete this tip, that is 5
minutes of preparation time and 45 minutes of 'Action
Time'.

Total 'Focus Time' means; No distractions, No internet, No
mobile, No email, No people, absolutely nothing that will

distract you. Sounds like I am telling you to lock yourself away in a concrete cell. Yes I am, well as close as you can get to that. You really do need to have total focus for this to work and to set you off on the right foot for the rest of the book.

Here's what you are going to do during the 5 minutes of preparation time;

- Get yourself a countdown timer, don't use the one on your phone unless you turn it onto flight mode first (flight mode stops all incoming communications)
- Remember no internet, no phone calls, no distractions
- Somewhere comfortable to sit
- Lots of plain paper
- 2 – 3 pens / pencils

For the next 45 minutes, without referring to any other bits of paper, laptop, emails etc, list absolutely everything you need to action in your life. N.B. You might want to do this separately, either totally focused on your business life or totally focused on your personal life; or as a combined effort which is preferred as it is easier to open up your mind totally this way without having to filter first.

You will find for the first 15 minutes you will easily list most of your current projects and tasks (your reactive stuff). See if you can break all of these down into actionable items, but that can always be done at a later time, the key is to get everything out. The magic happens in the 15 – 45 minutes section, this is where your mind will wander and it will feel like you are emptying every little bit of memory from your brain (your proactive stuff).

Keep going for the full 45 minutes until the timer goes off even if there is a 5 – 10 minute gap with no writing going on. Keep going because every now and again you will think of something else and that will spark a flow of more actionable items. You should feel totally drained of everything in your head by the end of 45 minutes.

Take Action: *Set the timer to 45 minutes. Hit start. Let the pen flow. Once you have created this list, this should be ABSOLUTELY EVERYTHING on your to do list. Go through the list and first group them into similar tasks, i.e. All the* phone calls together. Next put a time frame against every item in minutes. Then go through the list again and write whether it needs to be done in the next 30 days, 60 day or 90 days. Finally go through the list of 30 days and 60 days and ask 'will this still be a viable to do task in 90 days and adjust the list as necessary. If it fits outside of your next 90 days, schedule in your calendar and revisit in the next 75 days, but for now remove it as it will only clutter the tasks to hand. Move everything apart from the next 30 days to the 'Not To Do' list (see the next tip).

Tip 5 - Create A 'Not To Do List'

Having a 'Not To Do' list, does not mean you are not going to do it, it just means not at this moment as you need to focus on the next 30 days.

A 'Not To Do' list should consist of all your projects that if they were not done in the next 30 days would not be detrimental to the business. By putting these on your 'Not To Do' list, it removes them from your desk, from your mind but not from the business.

Tip 6 - Elimination vs. Organisation

Often you will spend the majority of your time trying to organise all of your tasks to fit in with your busy schedules. Every day you will sort things into piles (or piling systems as I like to call them), you will shuffle, reshuffle and shuffle again, trying to decide between what you like doing vs. what needs doing and you will often switch from one task to another.

What you need to do is go on a 'Task Diet'! What do I mean by this? Instead of organising every task on your plate, like an 'all you can eat buffet', eliminate the tasks that will not get you to your target weight! Elimination can be a powerful tool in your arsenal of ideas.

By eliminating, you are not necessarily getting rid of tasks, you are merely going on a diet and eliminating them from being in front of you right now, when they don't need doing for 30+ days. 'Eliminate' them if they are not part of your goals or 'Delegate' others to eat the foods (tasks) that will not be good for your health (business). This will free you up to do the things that matter most RIGHT NOW!

When you eliminate a task, you want to be asking yourself

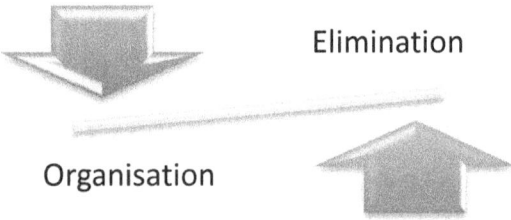

Elimination

Organisation

these three questions;

1. Do I (emphasis on 'I') need to deal with this task in the next 30 days?
2. Is completing this task imperative to me to reach my goals?
3. Am I the best person to deal with this task 'Right Now'?

If you answered 'No' to any of these questions, then you need to look at eliminating this task from your list right now and potentially delegating or outsourcing this to someone else.

Take Action: *Take a look at your piling system of tasks and create a diet plan to suit your weight (business) needs.*

Tip 7 - Add Learning To Your Daily Routine

You know what you need to do to get your life under control, but it seems like such a mammoth task. Ask yourself this. If you could spend 6 full days totally devoted to 'learning' how to rid yourself of this 'Fire Fighting' behavioural habit you are in, do you think you could succeed? I'm guessing you are saying 'YES'.

Then by just spending 12 minutes per day totally focused on learning new skills (that means no distractions whatsoever, turn off phones, put up a 'Busy' sign on the door, for just 12 minutes per day) that's it, that's all you need to do to succeed!

Reading one section of this book per day including the 'Take Action' section might be the starting point, but there is also a wealth of knowledge out there on the internet or in books for these 12 minutes per day. That is all it will take to get you that 6 days of totally focused time you said yes to earlier.

What?... How did you get to that? Well... 12 minutes per day (Monday – Friday Only) = 1 hour per week = 48 hours per year (allowing 4 weeks holiday) = 6 days of untapped learning. It's the long term vision approach that makes this happen. Just 12 minutes per day for 6 full days of learning at your own pace too... 'Cool, sign me up' I hear you saying.

Hmmm sounds interesting put that way. So how should I spend those 12 minutes? Spend 10 minutes of learning a topic that will move you forward and 2 minutes of journaling / 'Taking Action', that's it. You can learn a topic by reading a chapter of a book, watching a video, listening to a podcast or surfing the internet, whatever you choose, ensure the content matches your needs, goals and vision.

You are not attempting to master a complete topic in one go. For example if you were looking at communication skills as a topic, just focus each 12 minutes per day on a specific aspect to do with communication skills, e.g. communicating across generations, listening skills or dealing with conflict. As each 12 minutes progresses, you will be building up your overall communication skills knowledge.

This bite size learning is the magic 'Key to Success'. Imagine if you had 10 staff that all followed this 12 minutes per day, that's 60 days of learning and development. What would that do for your business? What about if they did 12 minutes in the morning and 12 minutes in the afternoon?   ONE HUNDRED AND TWENTY DAYS OF FOCUSED LEARNING DEVELOPMENT! If we really think about it, we can all find 12 minutes per day.

The key to this though is consistency. It is not worth doing it half heartedly or some days yes, some days no, it is something that you need to commit to. The learning you achieve from this bite size schedule will improve your performance, get implemented into the business and will deliver RESULTS.

You need to journal in your diary every day and everything you learnt in those 10 minutes (remember the 2 minutes are for journaling). Do this consistently and you have a traceable measure of success, but it also ensures you are committed to the process.

12 minutes is not long at all if you want to make a difference in your life. Think about this as an example; If you want to run four seconds faster in a 400 metres race in four years time then, if you actually broke down the difference in time down into bite size chunks you would only need to improve by the following...

All you need to do is improve by 1 second a year for the next 4 years, that's $1/12^{th}$ of a second a month or $1/52^{nd}$ of a second a week. Could you run 400 metres $1/52^{nd}$ of a second faster next week if you train every day for 12 minutes a day starting today?

That's the power of bite size development. Don't focus on four seconds, don't focus on one second, don't even focus on $1/12^{th}$ of a second, focus 12 minutes per day and improve your performance by $1/52^{nd}$ next week. It's the same for your learning development. The results will speak for themselves over the next four years.

Take Action: Decide if you are ready to commit to 12 minutes per day. Decide what topics would be most beneficial to learn during these 12 minutes of focus. Once you master 12 minutes per day, then think about 2 x 12 minutes per day, once in the morning and once in the afternoon... that's 12 days of development a year. Finally master 2 x 12 minutes, then go for the ultimate... 3 x 12 minutes per day... That gives you the equivalent of 18 days of development a year. What is unique is the more you develop your skills, the more you improve your performance, which in turn creates more time to do the things you want to do.

Tip 8 - Time Blocking

You generally 'Block Time' in your diary for meetings, but I wonder if you 'Block Time' in your calendar for every project / task / planning session etc? I'm guessing not. That's ok right now, but when you fully understand the power of 'Time Blocking', I know you will instantly switch to this way of getting things done.

'Blocking Time' in your diary allows you to have a 'Focus Time' to work on a project. When you block a meeting in your diary, you turn up and focus on the meeting, not what is going on outside the room (hopefully).

It is the same for Blocking Time for your projects and tasks. I am using 'Block Time' to write this book. Every day for six weeks I have blocked 2 hours of my day to writing this book. During these 2 hours of Blocked Time I have been totally focused on the book and not what is going on around me. That's how I wrote this book from start to finish in less than six weeks.

I knew I needed about 60 hours to complete the book. If I just tried to find that time as and when I could in my diary I knew it would never get written. Yet if I set a goal with a focused time frame (six weeks) and broke that down into daily (working week) 'Blocked Time', then in 6 weeks I would have completed the project. And yes I did it!

People were not able to book me for a coaching session during this 'Block Time' and I set my environment up so I also had no other distractions during this 'Block Time', and low and behold, book written from start to finish in six weeks.

'Blocking Time' is one of those golden nuggets of business life. I did an exercise with a coaching client who had so many projects he needed to complete in a 30 day period. After listing all the projects, scoring them, basically all the tips in this book, we then went and blocked his diary for every single minute of his business day. I am sure you can guess the results... Total Focused Blocked Time = Results.

If people know that you 'Block Time' for everything you do, guess what, they will then ensure they request your time in the same way, rather than just showing up to your desk with a pile of 'Fire Fighting' tasks, they would schedule a 'Blocked Time' with you. 'Block Time' could be just 15 minutes. Later in the book you will see the software tool I use to 'Block Time' for introductory conversations (15 minutes) or 1:1 coaching sessions (60 minutes). Block time to do the most important tasks first!

Take Action: Look at your calendar, look at your projects, look at the time slots available, and look how long each project will take. Then block out time in your diary and enter the details of each project in your diary.

Tip 9 - Cucumber Process

You don't eat a whole cucumber without slicing it up into smaller slices (well at least you shouldn't be seen doing that), the same should go for your projects.

When you look at your projects, look how each project can be divided into smaller chunks (tasks), then divide them into even smaller chunks (tasks), until each chunk (task) takes no more than 50 minutes to totally complete (more on this in a moment).

If you have a project that will take six months to complete, break it down in 26 mini weekly projects and 130 daily bite size tasks (based on a working week 26 x 5=130), then all you need to do is complete 1/130th per day and your project will complete on time.

Take Action: *Slice and dice your tasks until they are achievable to complete in 50 minutes. Once you have your tasks in 'achievable' focused 50 minute slices follow the next tip.*

Tip 10 - The 50:10 Formula & The 18:12 Concept

If you could ever write a mathematical formula that would guarantee things get done, you deal with projects one by one and still have time for those little things that need doing, you break and refresh regularly, and you develop your skills on an ongoing basis, then this formula is it...

50:10 + 18:12 = Results

This tip alone will be one of the biggest game changers for you. This tip blends a number of tips into one awesome 'super tip'. The 50 minutes part of the 50:10 formula is a 'Total Focus' time to concentrate on one particular task. The 10 minutes part of the 50:10 formula allows you to catch up with team members, check emails or do those little things that need doing that normally distract you from your main focus.

The 18 minutes part of the 18:12 formula is for that all important break, be it a coffee/tea or an H_2O refill break. Whatever it is get up and walk away from your desk... refresh and recharge your cells.

Now the 12 minutes part of the 18:12 formula is to work on your future, this 12 minute section is for you to develop your skills, by dedicating 12 minutes of 'Total Focus' time to your personal development (x amount of times a day, depending on your routine).

The final hour is 40 minutes for any last minute tasks, and then the last 20 minutes are for preparing for the next day, making up the 40:20 part of a sub formula;

$$50:10 + 18:12 + (40:20)$$

I would even suggest going as far as having a countdown timer to hand to ensure you remain focused on your time keeping. You will be surprised how quickly the timer will go off, but at the end of each day you will also be surprised how much you have achieved. This book was nearly totally written using the 50:10 + 18:12 formula.

Break you day into the following routine:-

Key

50 = Work on Projects	10 = Share with others
18 = Coffee / Tea time	12 = Learning Boost
40 = Complete last minute tasks	20 = Plan for tomorrow

Example

09.00 10.00	10.00 11.00	11.00 11.30	11.30 12.30	12.30 13.30	13.30 14.30	14.30 15.30	15.30 16.00	16.00 17.00
50:10	50:10	18:12	50:10	Lunch	50:10	50:10	18:12	40:20

Adjust to fit your hours of work. In planning the 40:20 part of the day, ensure you use the 20 minutes part of the 40:20 formula to plan out all the 50:10 activities for the following day.

Take Action: Decide if this full formula is for you... If it is, waste no time in getting this working for you. If it isn't don't ignore it, just follow the next tip. Use a timer to control the time switches as when you are completely focused it is easy to get carried away. Do stop at each switchover point as this will confirm you are on track to succeed.

Tip 11 - Two Hour Chunks

If you see the benefit of Tip 10, sticking to the full day of the 50:10 + 18:12 formula can appear to be really challenging at first although as time goes on this will become easier. So to break you into the routine, first just start with a two hour chunk and deliver 2 x 50 minute sessions of 'Total Focus' time with 2 x 10 minutes of sharing with others time.

You will be amazed how quickly the 50 minute sessions go by, but what you will quickly realise is the amount of work you will get done during this 2 hours of focus time. Once you see the power of this 50:10 formula, raise your game and step it up to (2x) 50:10 + (1x) 18:12 + (1x) 50:10, that will fill up your morning or afternoon. Keep raising your game until you are able to fill your day with the 50:10 + 18:12 + 40:20 formula.

Take Action: *Firstly commit to the first two hour session, followed by stepping up your game one step at a time until you reach the full day formula. Make sure you have two 50 minute projects / tasks ready to complete.*

Tip 12 - Stacking System

Stacking is very similar to blocking. In blocking you set a time period to focus on specific projects / tasks. In stacking you look to 'stack' 'and block' similar projects together so you are more in the zone for those activities, e.g. If you block 3 phone calls into your week, try stacking where possible so you have a focus phone time, or if you have 2 or more preparation times, try stacking these together so you can have a morning or afternoon of 'Stacked Blocked Time' and can benefit by being in the zone and at maximum performance.

Set days as a regular routine to stack tasks back to back, e.g. A coach would stack his clients on a certain day, a salesperson would stack all his cold calling on a certain day etc.

Take Action: Look at all the areas where you can 'stack' effectively. Create a 'stack schedule' and stick to it.

Tip 13 - 12 Tier Calendar Concept

You started at the beginning of these tips listing all of your projects, both now and in the forthcoming months. You've allocated time to them and you have identified if they need to be done in the next 30 – 90 days and what needs to be done later in the year.

Before long you will look round and wonder where did that time go? You knew you had been busy, but you had really wanted to get this aspect of your business launched and now you don't know when you can fit that in... Sounds familiar?

A really great strategy is to map out your whole year from an overall perspective with monthly goals and targets. Using your 30 days + list starting one month from now, (you need to clear your next 0 – 30 days tasks you identified first for this to work) plan out what developmental projects you want to work on each and every month.

That means the previous months project needs to be wrapped up, sealed and delivered. To ensure you don't overrun and stop the progress of the following months, make sure your projects fit into monthly timeframes. If not, break them down even further so they fit into one month timeframes only.

In order for this to succeed you need 'realistic' time frames for these projects, and to be totally focused on that project for that month. That means really understanding the direction of your company, understanding the areas that you need to develop, but also understanding that it can't all be done at once. Make sure you schedule these to fit in with the monthly timeframes that are achievable by you and the business.

As an example, the '12 Tier Calendar Concept' I am working to whilst writing this book is as follows. Each month (Tier) I have a 'Total Focus' on completing one Tier at a time. It starts with the eBook and what is needed to launch the eBook, then in Tier 2 I continue expanding the eBook and transform it into the physical book. Tier 3 will see me record the audio version of the book. Tier 4 the DVD of the book. Tier 5 the Monthly Online Programme etc;

Tier 1	Tier 2	Tier 3	Tier 4
eBook	Book	Audio Programme	DVD Programme

Tier 5	Tier 6	Tier 7	Tier 8
Monthly Online Programme	Online Coaching Programme	3 Month Online Programme	Mastermind Group

Tier 9	Tier 10	Tier 11	Tier 12
1 Day Seminar & Networking	Speaking	3 Day Residential Seminar	5 Day Residential Seminar

Now you can take that a step further by adding in specific tasks for each Tier. It is very much like project planning, but just at a high level, so you know what the next months coming focus will be about and how anything you are doing this month can tie into next month and the overall bigger picture.

Tier	Tier 1	Tier 2
Project	eBook	Book
Task 1	Narrow Target Market	Convert eBook Into Book
Task 2	Research Compelling Topic	Build Lead Generation For Launch
Task 3	Compile Chapters	Create Compelling Campaign
Task 4	Write eBook	Automate Campaign
Task 5	Build Landing Page	Market Launch eBook & Book

Each month you have a focus project to complete. Each month you get results. Results give you the motivation to strive forward. Striving forward gets you to your destination. Before long all your plans for the year are no longer dreams... They are a reality!

Take Action: Start with the end in mind and create a 12 Tier Calendar Concept for your business either at a high focus level or in depth task level.

Tip 14 - W.I.G.

A W.I.G. is... put simply, a **'Wildly Important Goal'**! (Acknowledgement to Stephen R Covey).

How does a W.I.G. fit in with dealing with 'Fire Fighting'? This is how I see it. There are a number of ways to use a W.I.G. in your day to day life, but first let's fully understand what a W.I.G. really is. What do we mean about 'Wildly Important Goals'? A 'Wildly Important Goal' is ONE goal that above all else will substantially move you forward in the right direction. It is so critical to the success of your business it deserves the title 'Wildly Important Goal'.

It is not a complete project or a task, but merely one goal that MUST be completed... It might be an important call to a client, it might be writing a proposal, it might be communicating a vision, whatever it is, it is 'WILDLY IMPORTANT' to you and or the business.

Daily W.I.G. – Personal

You should set yourself (preferably the night before) ONE W.I.G. that no matter what happens, you will not leave work the next day before completing it. So make sure your

W.I.G. is not 4 hours long, you want to keep this as simple as you can, but the key as I have said many a time already in this book is consistency and 'Taking Action'.

Who would be holding you accountable for this W.I.G.?... You! So you might want to share your W.I.G. with a colleague for additional motivation and accountability. I share my W.I.G.s with a strategic business colleague, who in turn keeps me motivated and accountable and I in turn do the same for him, so it is a 'Win, Win' situation where we both succeed.

So what can this really do for you? What would it look like as a bigger picture? If you could complete 240 'WILDLY IMPORTANT GOALS' do you think you and the business will be in a better place? Well 1 W.I.G. a day = 5 per week = 240 per year (5x48 allowing for holidays), not bad for just completing 1 W.I.G. per day? However unless you consistently deliver 1 W.I.G. per day, you will not see the results at the end of the year.

Weekly W.I.G. – Team

Now let's raise this to the next level... Let's get your whole team involved. What if... you had 10 team members, who all delivered a daily W.I.G. we're not talking about 240 WIGs per year now, we're talking about 2,400 W.I.G.s per year, traceable, evidenced and auctioned! That's the beauty of the W.I.G. in action.

Why don't you take this a step further, let's create a W.I.G. CULTURE in the office, where every week, the group meet up for 15 minutes (maybe first thing on a Monday morning), to discuss briefly how their W.I.G.s went last week and what their W.I.G.s are for this week. That is every week 50 'WILDLY IMPORTANT GOALS' being completed for the organisation with just 10 people and a team who all hold themselves accountable to deliver.

You can even introduce W.I.G. BUDDY'S who daily hold their buddy colleagues accountable to completing their W.I.G.s. Having a buddy doubles the chances of success for the individuals as well as the organisation. When I talk with my W.I.G. buddy, not only does it double the chances of success, we always uncover other opportunities to increase the value of the W.I.G.

Monthly WIG – Department

Now if you have 5 teams of 10 people in your department and once a month you meet to discuss your teams W.I.G.s for the month, you are looking in excess of 12,000 completed W.I.G.s for the year around 1,000 per month, not bad for just 50 people.

With everyone focused on delivering one W.I.G. each and every day, before long you will not only see increased performance but also high levels of motivation within the department.

Take Action: Create a W.I.G. Culture as a Daily W.I.G. and if you have a team as a Monthly W.I.G. If you believe at the moment that a daily W.I.G. is too much to handle, then just create a weekly W.I.G. instead, that is still 52 goals per year tracked, evidenced and completed... W.I.G.s just cause you to 'Take Action' and 'Taking Action' gets you RESULTS.

Tip 15 - Magic Formula 10 − 7 = 3

This tip allows you to really focus on what's important. When you have lots of projects on the go knowing where to start first can be a challenging task. This simple formula will solve all these issues.

$$10 - 7 = 3$$

So how does this work?

List your top 10 projects you need to focus on right now, numbering them 1 – 10. Next put them into priority order with the most important at number 1. Recheck your top 10 to ensure you are absolutely happy that they are in the right order.

Fold the sheet between priority 3 & priority 4. Then rip along the fold line and dispose of the bottom 7 projects (4 – 10). This takes away the clutter that is stopping you from progressing with 'Total Focus and Optimal Performance'. Now only work on the remaining 3 projects (1 – 3) as this focuses you on the three things that matter most.

When these top 3 projects are completed, rewrite the list from scratch. Do not go back to the original list and use 4 – 10, but start the list all over again from the beginning and repeat the formula $10 - 7 = 3$. Projects might have changed, priorities might have changed order, so it is important not to follow the previous list and to rewrite from the beginning.

You can do the same for the tasks of a project, i.e. List the 10 most important tasks of that project and run the formula $10 - 7 = 3$. The beauty of this tip is the focus it brings to completing the most important tasks first.

Take Action: Start with creating a project list and using the magic formula 10 - 7 = 3. When you get success with your projects, scale it up to your task lists.

Tip 16 - One Page Plan

You sit down at your desk, there are projects piled high on your desk, you know you need to do a lot of work today, but where do you start? Sounds familiar?

Let's look at where this possibly went wrong and put a structure in place to correct this. This really went wrong the minute you arrived at work with no clear focus on what needed doing that day. You knew you had to do a bit of this project a bit of that project but the lack of clarity meant you wasted time and most probably spent the day 'Fire Fighting' instead.

So how can you overcome this? Firstly, creating a daily 'One Page Plan' will ensure you focus completely on the top three tasks for that day and complete these before you start on anything else, or get distracted by anything else.

Secondly, you should create your 'One Page Plan' as the last task of the previous day, that way when you come into work the next day you know exactly what you need to do before any distractions and before you open up your email and get side tracked.

So what should go into your one page plan? You can download your 'One Page Plan' at www.FireFreeWorkDay.Com/OnePagePlan where you will see a full page 'One Page Plan' which you can either copy or download as many times as you need or create your own.

Let's talk about the structure of your 'One Page Plan'. Start this 'One Page Plan' the day before you want to be successful. There's no point coming into work without 100% clarity on what you need to do, otherwise the 'swarm' of business colleagues will 'without mercy' take up all of your time.

Your 'One Page Plan' should be simple enough to complete in 10 minutes and have the relevant sections that state;

Firstly, start by listing your top 3 projects you need to work on... TOP THREE not FIVE.

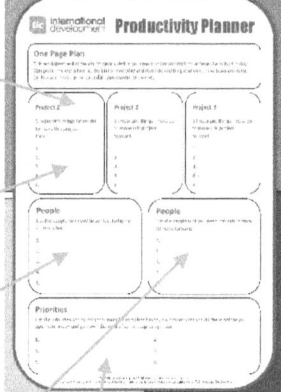

Now list the 3 - 5 most important things you MUST DO to move each of these projects forward. Have absolute clarity on what these are.

Secondly, list the people you need to contact in each of these projects (by contact I mean either in person or via phone or email), that will ensure the project moves forward.

Thirdly, list the people who you need something from, it might be a response to an email you sent or a piece of work that adds to your project etc. Above all you need this person to give you what you need in order for you to fulfil your end of the project.

Finally, list the priorities that must be completed that next day no matter what. These are the priorities that if not completed will cause delay or seriously hinder the progress to the projects.

Now, it's time to put the magic into this 'One Page Plan'. Providing you have planned this out carefully the day before you want to succeed, then when you leave work that night, clear your desk of any distractions. Distractions might be paperwork, magazines, projects.

When you arrive at work the next day, the only thing that should be visible to you is your 'One Page Plan'. Before you turn on your computer... yes even before you turn on your computer, look at your 'One Page Plan' and decide if you even need your computer on for the things you listed on your 'One Page Plan'. If you do need your computer on, turn it on but DO NOT open your email yet.

Did I say DO NOT open your email? Yes I did. You see, the minute you open your email, you start working on other peoples agendas, when what you know you need to work on is YOUR agenda. Your email is just an excuse for other people to distract you from what needs doing. Stick to the 'One Page Plan'!

Unfortunately, in order to contact the people you need to contact on your 'One Page Plan' or the people who you need something from you might have to check your email, but here is the deal. If this is the case, when you open your email, ONLY search for the people on your list, and do not get side tracked by peeping at what else might be in your inbox.

Now I know how difficult it will be, but if you really want this 'One Page Plan' to work, then you have to find a way to avoid being sucked into your email. An option is when opening up your email (maybe better if set up the day before) is just to have it filtered (Arranged By) to 'FROM' instead of 'DATE' and enter in the search inbox the person with whom you want to connect with. That way you remain focused and do not get drawn into other emails that will distract you from the 'One Page Plan'.

The key of the 'One Page Plan' is that it is simple enough to understand, yet powerful enough to clarify what needs to happen, by who and when. It needs to be accessible enough to keep with you and have a step by step layering of actions to complete, that all lead to your end goals.

Tip 17 - Frog Process

If you ask most people to eat a frog first thing in the morning, they would not like doing it. Chances are they would not like doing it later in the day either, but that is besides the point. I can't say I have actually tried this, but just the thought of it is turning my stomach right now. Brian Tracy talks about this in depth in his book 'Eat That Frog'.

If the first thing you did everyday was to eat a frog, you most probably won't find anything worse that you need to eat that day and that is the same for your projects and tasks. There will always be a task or project you don't like doing.

If you were to deal with the task you least like to do (N.B. We are talking about the ones that are on top of your lists but you don't like doing), then the rest of your day will only get better. If you keep putting it off because you don't like doing it, then you will get to the end of the day and it will still be left on your list to do, and now it will become 'Urgent & Important' and you will be doing everything you can to put it off.

Take Action: Identify daily what are your frogs? What do your frogs look like?... It might be cold calling, accounts or filing. Turn yourself into 'Prince Charming' and 'Kiss That Frog' and start getting used to eating your frog first thing in the morning. That way the rest of your day will always be full of nice foods (projects and tasks).

Tip 18 - Big Rocks, Little Rocks – Pint of Beer

I first came across this concept many years ago watching the late Stephen R Covey video where he actually demonstrated this process using a bucket and rocks to demonstrate the concept. It is worth finding on YouTube.

This is my interpretation of this concept and how it applies to 'Fire Fighting'. You start with a bucket, some large rocks, medium sized rocks, small rocks, pebbles and sand. If you put the items in any random order, the chances are that when you try to get everything into the bucket, they would end up sitting higher than the top of the bucket.

It's the same with your projects... When you have lots of projects and try to do all of them at the same time, flicking from one to another, doing different size tasks at various parts of the day, you end up finishing the workday (your bucket) with not everything completed and projects overflowing to the next day.

However if you take the concept of starting with the large rocks, followed by the medium rocks, the small rocks, the pebbles, giving a little shake around so they settle in the gaps formed by the larger rocks, then do the same with the sand, smoothing off to a perfect flat top, they would all fit in.

That is the same for your projects... If you start your day with the large projects, after tea work on some middle sized projects, after lunch the smaller projects and finish the day off with the all the little bits and pieces then... you could smooth off your day and you could still find room to pour in liquid, which would seep in through the sand, around the pebbles and in between the rocks, getting even more done.

The moral of this story is, when you start with the big projects (big rocks and medium rocks) and gradually work down in size (small rocks, pebbles and sand), then when you get to the end of the day and it appears you have completed everything (smooth top of bucket)... Here's the best bit... you can still have room for the liquid in this case 'A Beer or Glass of Wine'!

Take Action: Take a look at your workload, decide what are your Big Rocks, Medium Rocks, Small Rocks, Pebbles and Sand and then set about this strategy to fit it all into your bucket (your work day) and when you succeed, go and treat yourself to a pint of beer or a glass of wine.

Tip 19 - Gold Coins

Imagine a tennis court scattered with gold coins, silver coins and bronze coins. You have 2 minutes to collect as many coins as you can carry in this given time, the chances are you can only carry about $1/3^{rd}$ of the total coins in the tennis court.

How would you progress? Would you pick up all the coins nearest to you ensuring you were full of coins by the 2 minutes? Would you pick up as many coins as possible nearest to you, and then if time permits get rid of bronze or silver coins to replace them with gold coins or would you just go looking for gold coins?

Let's look at the business scenario for this... If those coins were ideas, projects or tasks, eliminating the coins that don't matter is a far more effective strategy to manage your time than organising them by collecting as many as possible then sorting through them. When you are totally focused on the gold coins, nothing else will matter. If you get to the end of your day and have collected every gold coin in sight and there is still time left then go and focus on the silver coins. But, initially stay focused ONLY on the gold coins of your business.

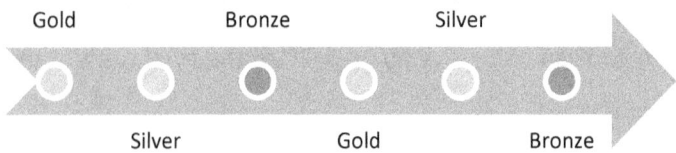

Gold   Bronze   Silver

Silver   Gold   Bronze

Take Action: Can you easily identify what are your gold, silver and bronze coins in your business? Create a list of these business coins, then only focus on the gold coins. Each day recreate the list as a silver coin yesterday might be a gold coin today.

Tip 20 – Project & Task Debt

If you have ever been in debt when you have lots of people chasing you for money, not only does it become overwhelming and stressful wondering if that next call is someone chasing you for payment but it also takes a toll on your emotional level, making you feel drained and exhausted.

You tend to deal with these debts erratically, dealing with the person shouting the loudest at any given time, just to get them off your back, but that also puts other plans further behind schedule.

It's the same for 'Project and Task Debts'. As the 'Projects and Tasks Debts' keep building up, you tend to 'Fire Fight' by dealing with the loudest shouter first, often at the demise of all of your other projects and tasks.

Take time to list and sort out all of your 'Projects and Tasks Debts'. That means knowing what the debt is, how long it will take to get out of debt (hours not pounds) and strategising a plan to deal with these debts using some of the techniques already discussed in this book. This will greatly benefit your time, stress and health as well as ensuring you get results for your business.

I did an exercise with a coaching client who was overwhelmed and over stressed with his day to day work life. We first took a look at his 'Wheel of Life' and calculated how many hours he was spending vs. how many he wanted to spend, on work related projects. We then took a look at all of his debts (projects & tasks), listed them all and put a time amount against each debt.

That's when the lights when on, when he realised his debts completely took over his life, that if he only worked on his debts it would be more hours than he could physically work whilst still keeping a work / life balance. Yet he was still trying to do lots of other things and was wondering why at the end of each week he was left with more projects and tasks than he started the week with, and why his stress and frustration levels were through the roof.

Knowing your 'Debts' and the impact they are having on you on a day to day basis is essential if you want to move forward. In the case above, we took a close look at each debt, decided whether they were gold, silver or bronze debts and quickly eliminated the debts that were just causing a strangle hold on the business.

Take Action: What is EVERY ONE of your 'Debts' (projects and tasks)? List every debt, put a completion time against each one and then decide if they are a gold, silver or bronze

debt. Now decide upon a strategy to fit this into your work
life balance by eliminating bad debts.

Tip 21 - Multitasking Myth Busted

Some people say they a good at multitasking, let's see if we
can prove them wrong and that focusing on one thing at a
time will get better and quicker results.

Here's an activity to try with some colleagues. Find a
partner, each partner has a piece of paper with three
columns drawn on it. On the word 'GO' both partners need
to simultaneously fill in the following;

1st column	2nd column	3rd column
odd numbers	months	even numbers
1 – 23	Jan – Dec	2 – 24

One partner (A) will ONLY be allowed to go DOWN the
columns completing each column as they go, the other
partner (B) will ONLY be allowed to go ACROSS the rows
completing each row as they go, each person will shout out
'DONE' each time they complete a column. Give it a go!

I'm guessing the results you got were that the person focused on the columns first style finished all three columns before the other person came in with a 'DONE, DONE, DONE' finale. So you see multitasking is not quicker.

Interestingly if each column had a monetary value, e.g. If each column was worth £1,000, then the column person (A) would have earned £3,000 and be able to earn more money before the row person (B) had earned a penny.

In this case would you prefer to get paid at the end of each column (project / task) and have time to complete more or in the last three actions? Does this prove that multitasking is not always the best option? Get focused on completing ONE project / task at a time.

Take Action: Look at what you are currently multitasking... What could you do to focus on completing one project / task at a time, rather than multitasking?

Tip 22 - Malteser Process

I don't know about you, I am generally a one Malteser at a time person (if you haven't heard of them look them up). I like to peel off the chocolate and then suck on the honeycomb until it dissolves in my mouth. What has Maltesers got to do with 'Fire Fighting'?

If you were to fill your mouth with all the Maltesers or even a lot of Maltesers in one go, you wouldn't really enjoy the flavour. It's the same with your projects and tasks... When you tackle one project or task at a time, peeling back the layers of the project or task and enjoying the inner aspects of it, that's when you will truly relish the end result.

However most of the time I am guessing you are completing many many projects at a time, flicking from one to another and not really getting to enjoy any of them.

Take Action: What would be your Maltesers? How can you truly enjoy your Malteser? If you were to strip the outer edges off so you can get to the inner flavour, what would that look like? Treat each project / task as a Malteser, list them all and then complete them one at a time.

Tip 23 - Let Your Team Know About Your 50:10 Formula

We've talked about the 50:10 formula earlier in the book. This tip is to ensure you really impress upon your colleagues the impact they have on your 'Fire Fighting' capabilities.

Your colleagues are most probably some of the biggest distractions that cause you to end up 'Fire Fighting'. I doubt they constantly engage with you just to cause you to not be productive, in fact if they are constantly contacting you they most probably look up to you. But what they don't realise, as I am sure up until you have not told them, is the impact they are having on your productivity.

Let everyone know that from now on you work totally focused on your projects and tasks for 50 minutes 'Block Time' and they can contact you during your 10 minutes 'Block Time' refresher break. It is not always possible, but the easiest way is to keep to the hour clock, so that colleagues know to connect with you at the 0:50 (ten to) mark on the hour.

Unless the building is on fire, your team should know that you are only available at the 0:50 slot and for ten minutes only. You are not to be disturbed for anything that can't wait till the 0:50 mark, but during this 10 minute slot you will give them your total dedicated time. Create a culture of the same pattern amongst your colleagues. If everyone was head down focused for 50 minutes slots, what an amazing amount of work you could get through with no distractions.

If you need someone to answer the phones, switch the times around, so someone always has their 0:10 minute slot at a convenient time.

Take Action: Communicate in an effective way to your team, outlining not just the 'What & How' of this 50:10 concept, but more importantly the 'Why'. Explain how critical to your success they are in not disturbing you during your 50 minute focus time.

Tip 24 - ScheduleOnce

How many emails or calls does it take to confirm and schedule a date in your diary? One, two, four, eight? What about if you need to change it after it is scheduled, one, two, four, eight again?

Having a system that frees up more of your valuable time, will ensure you are able to put out the fires and keep them from re-igniting, allowing you to be more productive. If you are a busy professional who meets with many people you probably agree that managing your calendar is a big challenge. Is there a better way for people to get on your calendar with no hassle to you or them?

There is and it is called ScheduleOnce. ScheduleOnce is an online scheduling solution that works in tandem with your personal calendar. With ScheduleOnce you have a personal MeetMe link, for example meetme.so/richardabrahams.

People that click this link can immediately see when you are available and schedule time with you according to your exact rules and preferences.

ScheduleOnce will save you time and provide an outstanding scheduling experience for the people that want to meet with you. When you start using ScheduleOnce you will receive compliments on how easy it was to schedule with you.

ScheduleOnce not only takes care of scheduling, it also handles cancellations and rescheduling - It is just like having a personal assistant, without having to pay the bill.

Take Action: *Try this for yourself and get a free trial offer on the* ScheduleOnce *website* www.scheduleonce.com *to try this for yourself. N.B. We do not get any commission from this company, we promote their services because we use them ourselves. If you would like to schedule a meeting with me, my calendar availability is at* meetme.so/richardabrahams.

Tip 25 – Time Splitting

Some of you might have more than one side of a business to focus on. If you have a number of sides to your business and you can't get them all, either flowing smoothly or off the ground, then 'Time Splitting' might work for you as it did for a recent coaching client.

A coaching client I am working with has three sides to his overall empire and each of them in their own right could be a separate business. There is a web design company, an eLearning company and a success company. The web design company was eating up the majority of his time as it was a reactive business with lots of deadlines, it was good for cash flow but not for the bigger picture. The eLearning company was a new business that he wanted to work on so it would become self supporting, but he knew his real passion was for the success company.

It became obvious in chatting this through with him, that the success business wasn't moving forward and there was never enough time left at the end of the week to work on it as he spent all of his time on the other two businesses.

So the strategy we came up with was visualising if he was a year down the line and everything was running how he wanted it to be, how many days would he be working on each business? With that visualised information we then set up a plan to 'Time Split' from now, to match the plan he had previously visualised.

He now has a clear focus of how his time is split between the different businesses, and ensures that he remains focused on the plan as it will ultimately (and is already) leading him to his desired outcome.

Take Action: If you have separate businesses or have a business that you want to get launched, agree a time split that you WANT to be working on in the future, then commit to that NOW. If you don't commit now, unfortunately the chances that you will still be doing the same thing a year from now are very, very high.

Tip 26 - Take Action, Acknowledge Results

We've talked about the 'Five Keys to Success' a number of times with 'Stage 4' being 'Take Action'. All through this book, actually every step of this book, there has been a section about 'Taking Action'.

'Taking Action' is the only way you will get results, so if you have read this book so far, and haven't yet 'Taken Action', that is either because you don't believe any of these strategies will work for you or you don't want these strategies to work for you.

However if you have 'Taken Action' and got results now is the time to acknowledge these results.

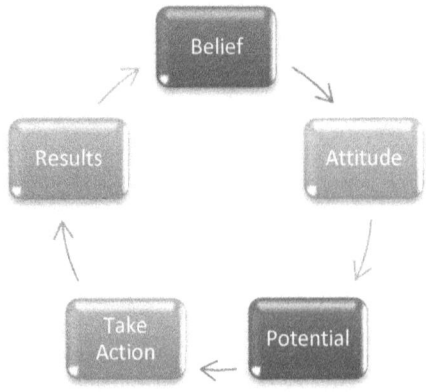

Why would you acknowledge results? When you get a result, that strengthens your **belief** that you are doing the right thing. It motivates your **attitude** and opens your mind to reach more **potential**, which in turn causes you to '**Take Action**' and hey presto... You get more **results** and so the cycle continues.

Sharing your results with colleagues and friends will also spark two reactions. You will feel a sense of pride and satisfaction as well motivating you to succeed even more. For your colleagues and friends, firstly they will feel great knowing you are being successful, secondly you will inspire them to believe that they too can reap the benefits of the 'Five Keys To Success' and extinguishing their own fires.

Take Action: You have to 'Take Action', that goes without saying. Look for some quick wins (results) that you can acknowledge that will inspire your belief to stretch yourself further.

Tip 27 - Set A Daily Reminder

You are going to be so engrossed in these new strategies that you won't know where time has gone. You will see lots of results, but you might find the day ending quicker than planned as you get more done.

Part of the 50:10 concept included a 40:20 section. The 20 is about preparing for the next day. By preparing for the next day you leave work with a clear understanding of what is in store for you when you next return. Also as you spend your evening resting and sleeping your subconscious mind will be working away gaining insights into the work it has to do tomorrow, giving you a head start.

We have previously spoken about 'Blocking Time' for projects and tasks and this is one of those times that blocking time is really useful. Create a daily reminder that blocks the last 20 minutes of every day and sends you a reminder so you can stop what you are doing and plan for tomorrow. The last 20 minutes is also a good time to use your 'One Page Plan' to organise your following day.

Wow it is all coming together, three strategies in one go... '50:10 Concept'... 'Block Time'... 'One Page Plan', even I am impressed.

Take Action: Block Time in your diary TODAY and everyday for the last 20 minutes of your working day. Use this time to plan for the next day.

Tip 28 - Email Time

Nowadays it is not unusual to get 200+ emails a day. People are sending emails and expecting responses like it was 'instant messenger'. Emails are becoming the catalyst to 'Fire Fighting' issues with people inundated with the endless supply of emails.

I've written about email filtering previously in the book to help keep your inbox from getting to full by filtering off the non essential emails and filing them before they even hit your inbox. N.B. You can still read them in the 'Unread Folder'.

What you need now is a way to ensure you stay in control of YOUR agenda and not end up on OTHER PEOPLES agendas. You see, the minute you open your email, unless you are totally focused on what you need to do when you open your email, other people are doing EVERYTHING they can to distract you from the task at hand.

They will use clever tricks like catchy subject lines, personal messages, flashy pictures or promises of changing your life. They will test and test their strategies until they come up with the one that will draw your attention away from what you are doing... and force you to be on THEIR agenda rather than YOUR agenda. N.B. Remember email is just a trap your colleagues use to keep you on THEIR agenda, not YOURS.

But you can be cleverer than them, because now you know that THEIR agenda is to take you away from YOUR agenda, you can stop them.

How?...

Firstly, you have to limit checking your email, so open it ONLY when you need to check it. Turn off the notification box as that instantly draw your attention away from the task at hand and remember they write catchy phrases to draw you in.

Secondly, only check your email 3 times per day. Once in the morning (as part of your 'One Page Plan'), next when you have completed everything on your 'One Page Plan' and finally in the afternoon, turn it off between these times to avoid any distractions.

Start letting people know that you only check your emails three times a day. That way you are educating them in how YOU want to handle YOUR emails, not how THEY want you to handle THEIR emails.

Finally, when you first open your email, only look for the people that relate to your 'One Page Plan' otherwise you will quickly end up on THEIR agenda and not YOURS.

I know how difficult, challenging and weird this sounds; turning your email off. But once you fully embrace this concept, I know you will be writing back to me saying what a game changer this is.

Once they know your style, they will generally only send you emails that are Not Urgent but Important (the type you can plan your time around), rather than the Urgent and Important (the type you find yourself 'Fire Fighting').

The Urgent and Important should really be dealt with either face to face or on the phone and if they know you work to a 50:10 rule, then they would have to schedule these allowing you to 'Block Time' to deal with these. You see how this works, you become the driver not the passenger. When you are the Driver you choose the direction.

Take Action: Firstly, go and turn off your email notification TODAY! Next make sure you have your 'One Page Plan' to hand when you first open up your email. Look for those people then turn it off again... NO PEEKING! Set a schedule, even 'Block Time' when you will look at your email. Finally tell everyone that you NOW only check your email 3 times a day, so if they need you urgently (and this book should be showing you that means there is a fire in the office) they find another way to contact you or book time with you.

Tip 29 - How Do You Know When You Are There?

This tip goes right back to the beginning of the book when you visualised what a 'Fire Free Work Day' would look like. I wrote about if you couldn't visualise what success in regards to your 'Fire Fighting' issues would look like, how would you ever know you are there?

I can't tell you exactly what it should look like to you, as it will be different to everyone, but you can look back at your 'Take Action' sections to see what you wrote. What I can tell you is, if you are looking back now over a period of time where you have been implementing the strategies, you will be feeling very proud of yourself, like the day you won an award at school or were acknowledged for good work.

I am not sure if you ever will be there as there will always be a 'Fire Fighting' situation looming in the future, but what I can tell you this. If you are consistently implementing these strategies, you will definitely be the one in the DRIVING SEAT and knowing exactly what needs doing, by when, to ensure the situation is dealt with effectively.

I believe another way you will know you are there is when you find yourself sharing these strategies and knowledge with others about how these tips have worked for you, what results you got and how they improved your life. When you start teaching other people how to extinguish their 'Fire Fighting' bad habits, then you have truly mastered your belief, attitude and potential.

Take Action: Start sharing these strategies with colleagues. Become a lifelong sharer of knowledge and educate all those around you. Choose one person right now that you feel will benefit from learning from you and tell them the story about your journey. Get them to go to the website www.FireFreeWorkDay.Com to download their own copy of the eBook, and share regular 'Fire Fighting' tips with them.

Tip 30 - Celebrate Your 1st Day

You've done so well, you are nearly at the end of the book, you've tried lots of new strategies and you have found the ones that really work well for you. Now it is time to celebrate!

Celebrate at the end of your first day, and every day then on, that you stay 100% focused trying these new strategies. Let the world know what it is doing for you personally, the more people you tell, the more they will motivate you further. Watch how quickly and infectious it will become when others are also following you and learning the secrets to a 'Fire Free Work Day'.

If a bad day creeps back in, don't panic, a Fire Marshal always tells you to walk not run... Take the same approach when a bad day creeps in, take stock of what has happened, realign your standards, reflect on the good days and bring the bad day back into alignment.

Take Action: Go and celebrate!!! Tell everyone you meet what you are up to, the struggles, the strategies and the successes. Watch how, when people ask 'how you are doing'? You respond 'I am loving life, I have finally got all my 'Fire Fighting' issues under control, I am in the driving seat of my own time and performance and I am getting more done, having more fun and taking control of my time everyday'. I bet one of the first words that comes out of their mouths is 'WOW' followed by, 'I'd like some of that too'! TELL EVERYONE YOUR SUCCESSES and relish their responses.

What Next?

The Next Steps

The next steps are really up to you. You need to decide if you are thirsty for more knowledge and if you want to improve your performance and your skills further. You need to make decisions about your future, your commitment to excel at everything you do. You need to take the bull by the horns and clearly define where you are going in life.

However, we are here to help you in any way we can to ensure you are successful. You can always drop us an email at info@tlcinternationaldevelopment.com where we would love to hear your stories and offer any guidance that we can. And if you have any testimonials to how this book changed the way you deal with 'Fire Fighting', we'd love to hear from you so please drop us an email. But remember we only open our emails three times a day!

Work, Rest, Play Balance

Time To Play

You've spent a lot of time reading and 'Taking Action' about how to put out the fires at work and 'How To Get More Done, Have More Fun And Take Control Of Your Time Today'. With this extra time you would have generated you need to now make 'Time To Play'.

You should spend some time writing a mission statement about how you will spend this 'Having More Fun' aspect of your lives. When you have more fun you will also become clearer about your personal and professional direction.

In order to stay fully on the ball at work, you need to also tap into inspiration outside the workplace. Every day after work you should take 20 minutes of physical exercise, e.g. Swimming, running, cycling, walking.

After a few weeks of consistent exercise you will find that it serves as a great recharger of your battery cells as well as allowing you to switch off from work and have 'Time To Play'.

In order to have 'Time To Play' you need to make sure the things that keep you awake at night or drag you down during the day are under control or eliminated from the equation. You also need to ensure you 'Block Time' for the things you normally leave to the last minute (if you have time) i.e. Holidays. By Blocking Time in advance for your holidays you give yourself a goal to aim for and the motivation to get there.

Finally always look for more ways you can save time so you can have more 'Time To Play', i.e. The amount of 'Online' time you spend each day is growing and growing. You could potentially save well in excess of an hour a day, by watching where you surf and where you get distracted by inviting adverts, articles or videos.

If you saved 1 hour per day on internet time, that is equal to 240 working hours per year (5 days per week x 48 weeks) that you could then spend on 'Time To Play'. On average if you get 20 days holiday a year that is like having an extra 1½ times your current holiday allowance each year.

Time To Rest

As well as 'Time To Play' being introduced into your life once again, you need to have 'Time To Rest'. The last time was most probably many years ago. By 'Time To Rest' I mean switching off and relaxing, not sleeping. Finding 'Time To Rest' is essential if you are to regain any balance in your life.

Relaxing after a busy day at work is a real challenge for most people, especially those who have been caught in the whirlwind of 'Fire Fighting'. If you don't find time to relax or time to recharge your cells then things like tiredness, fatigue and exhaustion are going to affect your life and you will see mistakes creeping into your work, frustration with your colleagues, lack of attention to detail in your projects and a number of other tendencies.

This will cause you more stress, more grief and ultimately end up with you working longer hours to compensate. I think you get the message.

When we look at really successful leaders we tend to see them as much in their work clothes as they are in their golf clothes or on the beach. Why? Because they have mastered the Work, Play, Rest balance. They know if they get this balance right they are likely to be more productive at work and they will inspire the people they connect with.

Rest days need to be rest days, play days need to be play days and work days need to be work days. Try to never mix the three together. That means on a rest day, turn off the phone, don't open your email and just focus on resting. Now rest will be different for most people. Rest might mean just chilling by the beach or reading a book (even a business book), but it must be relaxing to get the full benefit.

Work out a schedule for you that is the right balance of 'Rest Time' and then 'Block Time' in your diary. Think about a regular schedule, like working for twelve weeks then taking one week off and do it consistently, like clockwork, so you always have something to look forward to.

30 Day Challenge

You're on the home straight now and the finishing line is coming up fast. You've nearly read the whole of this book and I trust you have been trying new strategies along the way. If left to your own devices, so much can go wrong and fall by the wayside, especially if there is no commitment to improve or people to hold you accountable. What about if we set you a challenge?

What could you challenge yourself to? How about you create a 30 day challenge starting today? Each day, challenge yourself to achieve one thing and tell everyone about your challenges to bring them alive and make you committed and accountable.

So what could your 30 day challenge consist of? Maybe;

- Day 1 - Re-read one of your favourite tips from the book and take the relevant action.
- Day 2 - Clear your desk area of EVERY piece of loose paper.
- Day 3 – Teach someone else one of the strategies in this book.

Take Action: Create your own 30 day challenge. Set one achievable, but stretching challenge everyday and share it with everyone that matters in your life. Celebrate the success and if you have a glitch day, don't worry, panic or give up on your challenge... just refocus, re-engage and get back on target.

That's it! You're Done!

Thank You

Thank you for taking the time to read this book. I trust you have found many tips and strategies to help you grow. If you have any of your own cool tips, then send them to us at info@tlcinternationaldevelopment.com and when we run the second edition, we may add your tips (if they are good enough ☺).

Thank you so much for your support and look out for the supporting programmes that will add even more value to your 'Fire Fighting' issues;

www.FireFreeWorkDay.Com/Products

 Audio Programme

 DVD Programme

 Online Learning Programme

Richard Abrahams

CEO & Founder | TLC International Development

Author | Fire Free Work Day & Associated Product Suite

About The Author

I'm Richard Abrahams.

I am the proud Chief Executive Officer and Founder of TLC International Development, a company specialising in guaranteeing a **'Return On Investment'** for all of its clients through the development of individuals and businesses.

My goal is to deliver a 'Paradigm Shift' to the 'Training & Development' industry through our unique

TLC Approach™, which blends…

Training, Learning and Coaching into one innovative and inspiring programme that guarantees results for all who participate.

My passion is helping individuals and businesses achieve their personal and business goals. I strive to push the boundaries of what we currently know and do, I thrive on innovating new ideas and concepts that inspire others, I relish on unleashing the talents in individuals and businesses and I ensure what gets learnt, gets implemented and what gets implemented, GETS RESULTS!

If you are interested in finding out how our TLC Approach™ and our 3 x ROI Guarantee could benefit you, please visit www.tlcinternationaldevelopment.com and check us out!

Please also feel free to drop me a personal email telling me how this book has supported you and what 'Action' you took and the results you got.

richard@tlcinternationaldevelopment.com

Richard Abrahams

CEO & Founder | TLC International Development

Author | Fire Free Work Day & Associated Product Suite

About The Inspiration

I want to make a special note of thanks in getting this book published to Dean Jackson

Dean gave me the inspiration to write this book at his three day 'Breakthrough DNA Blueprint' marketing workshop that I attended. I highly recommend that you attend one of these.

Dean fell in love with Marketing as a young boy when he first realised that selling stuff on commission was way easier than renting himself out by the hour for a regular job...and he's never looked back.

Dean has carried that distaste for real work into his adult life, and has focused on a lifestyle centered approach to business using marketing as the ultimate lever to a life of freedom and fun.

Dean has been having killer conversations about marketing for over 15 years, and now you can hear them on his weekly podcast that he delivers with Joe Polish.

Go and have a listen at www.ILoveMarketing.Com, you'll be inspired!

Thanks Dean!

Future Books & Product Suites

Sign up to be notified as soon as they are released!

www.FireFreeWorkDay.Com/Future

The End... For Now!

Take

Action

Today!